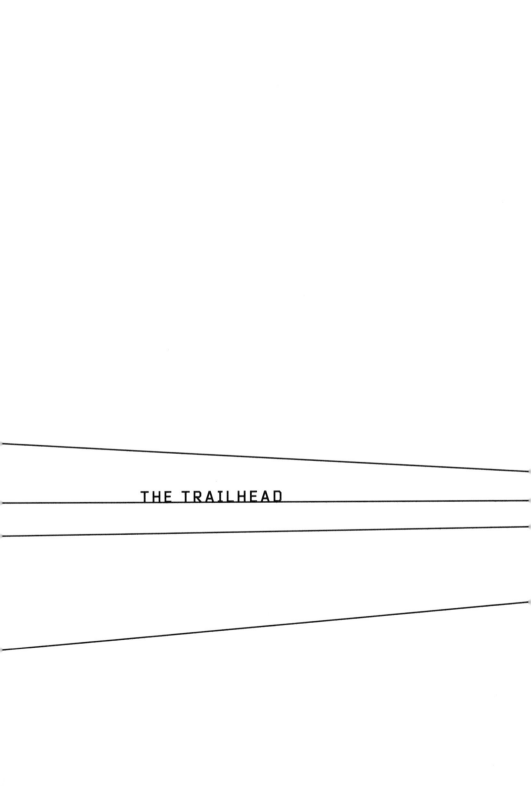

THE TRAILHEAD

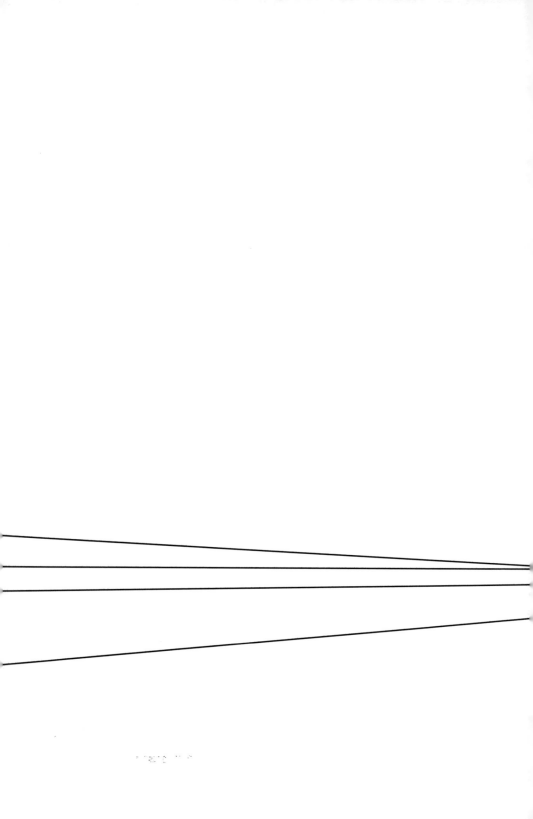

Kerri Webster

# the TRAILHEAD

Wesleyan University Press | Middletown, Connecticut

Wesleyan Poetry

Wesleyan University Press
Middletown CT 06459
www.wesleyan.edu/wespress
© 2018 Kerri Webster
Manufactured in the United States of America
Designed by Mindy Basinger Hill
Typeset in Sina

Library of Congress Cataloging-in-Publication Data

*Names*: Webster, Kerri, 1971– author.
*Title*: The trailhead / Kerri Webster.
*Description*: Middletown, Connecticut : Wesleyan University Press, 2017. |
    Series: Wesleyan poetry | Includes bibliographical references. |
*Identifiers*: LCCN 2017043088 (print) | LCCN 2017043317 (ebook) |
    ISBN 9780819578129 (ebook) | ISBN 9780819578112 (cloth : alk. paper)
*Classification*: LCC PS3623.E3974 (ebook) | LCC PS3623.E3974 A6 2017
    (print) | DDC 811/.6—dc23
LC record available at https://lccn.loc.gov/2017043088

5   4   3   2   1

Grateful acknowledgment is made to the editors of the following
    publications, in which some of the poems in this volume first appeared:
*Anthropoid*: "Hulls Gulch," "Winter Of (And I Took the Chemise Off)"
*At Length*: "The Night Grove"
*Better*: "Skins"
*BOAAT*: "The Spinster Project," "Of Deborah," "Wilderness, Poetry, Sex"
*Denver Quarterly*: "One Eye Dilated"
*Grimoire*: "On the Nature of Righteous Action," "Towards an Ethical
    Religiosity," "Reasonable Miracles," "The Trailhead," "Invert Sky," "Vanitas"
*Guernica*: "Corpse Flower"
*Los Angeles Review*: "This Is Manifest"
*Newfound*: "Solastalgia," "Swan/Not Swan"
*Poetry*: "Hermeneutics"

Gratitude to the Idaho Commission on the Arts for a grant that helped
in the writing of this book.

National
Endowment
for the Arts
arts.gov

This project is supported in part by an award
from the National Endowment for the Arts.

# CONTENTS

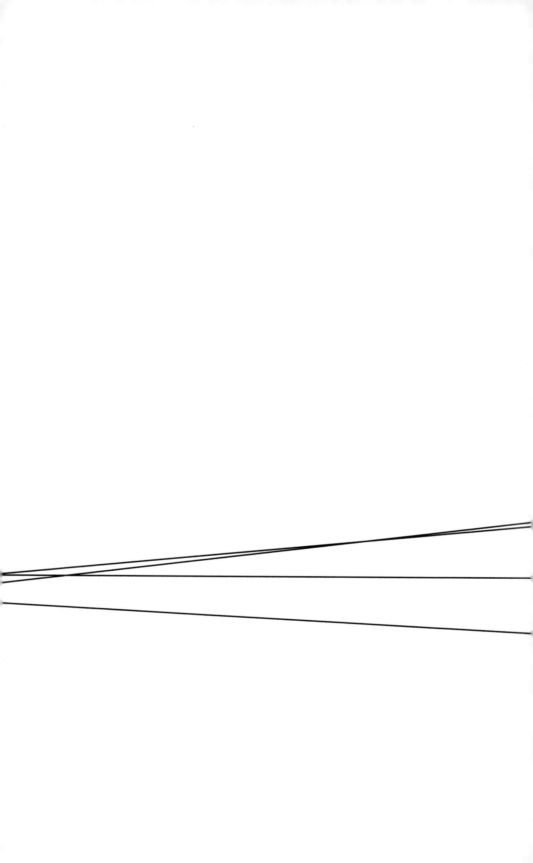

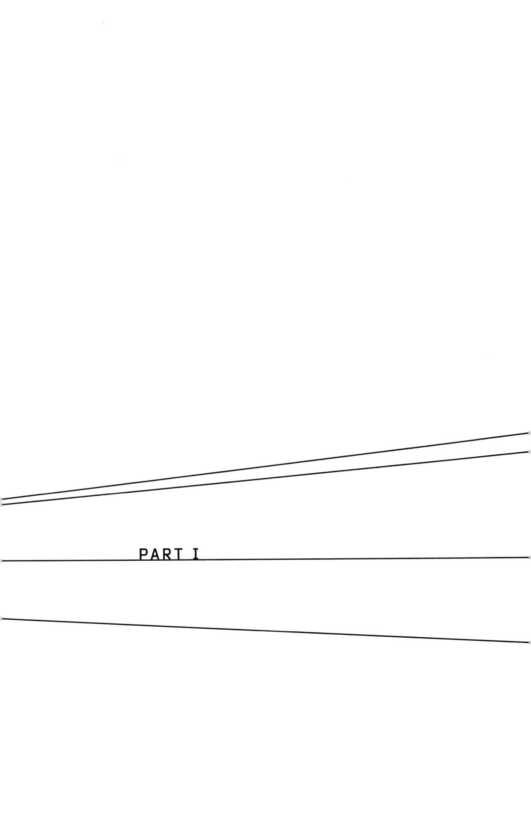

PART I

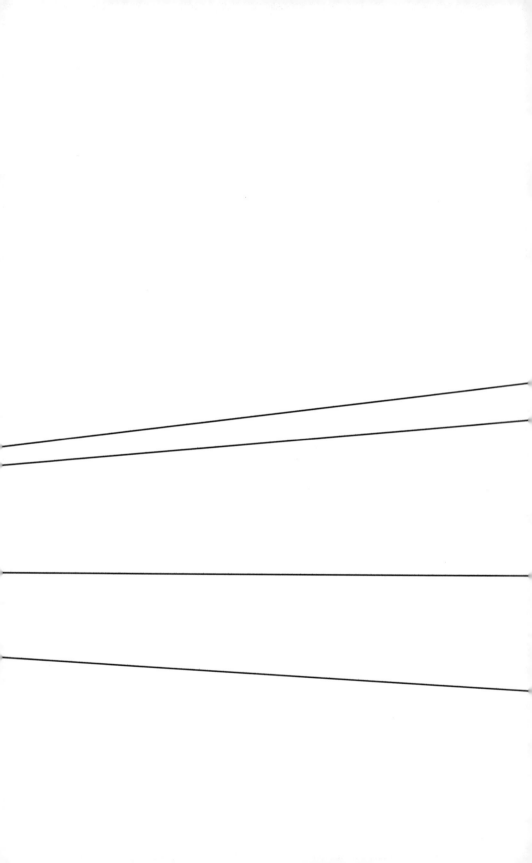

# HERMENEUTICS

All winter she's been growing more powerful.
Radiant, says the man at the bar.
Voluptuous, says the docent.
Nervy, says God.
All winter her soul has been juddering.
It feels like drinking gold flakes!
The word sleeps inside the stone.
The wind tongues the underside of the lake.
Inside the rifle scope of time, God
teaches her Grounding Techniques
through his emissary, a Certified Therapist.
Beetles bore their dirty traffic into pine trees.
God says, You cling to deixis
like a life raft. *Here*, you say. *Now*,
you say. *All winter*, you say, like it means
something, days crossed off your compulsive
calendar, wind tied to your wrist
like a pet. This dumb hunger for fixity!
I made your cells to shed, says God.
She bites her lip till it bleeds.
Who wouldn't immanentize the eschaton
if they could, build heaven on earth
in the backyard? She wouldn't, is who.
Day a slit-throated ewe.
To ground herself, she strips berries
from juniper bushes.
Well, says God, Alexander the Great
dyed his hair saffron. We are all
made fools in this world.

# HILL WALK

Come let us poison all the honeybees for we
are in world's dotage—insensible—and
seeing things: spectral migrations; unholy
gyres; squid that light up; a yew tree struck
by lightning, which must mean something;
a back lashed until it suppurates and comes apart
like what paper the wasps spit out; a blinded man
held in a cell for years for
what, for what—
and the river slivers the dark.
And someone says, *Cast him out at gates and let him*
*smell his way to Dover;*
and centuries pass; and then
someone says it again; and if
we are not cruel, perhaps it is only
because we are too tired to be cruel.
I dream hounds that bite my belly, teeth
to the softest skin. My needs grow simple
until nothing of me needs
redacting. I walk the hills by night;
I want to put them in my mouth.
There is an hour at which
the foothills silver—
if there are snakes, they are for sleeping.
I go where called.
*And cry these dreadful summoners grace?*
There is an hour at which all manner of dark
miracles appear—
like, foxes; or, shame; or,
the soldier's legs leave his body
and walk on by me;
or, strips of skin from off the man's back
half a world away
fly by my face
as ash—

and all birds are ghosts of the bird
I once drowned in a paper cup
after the cat tore it open but
it kept breathing. Tonight the gulch
eats tire rims and colored pencils, the gulch
eats foxes, and pulses
as we sleep, and as we sleep
the appetites continue, and what we harm
smells its way towards us.

# HULLS GULCH

Months from any tree becoming remotely fragrant yet one cannot remain in bed. What if, by the time things forsythia, we no longer recognize the flora, believe it's some sort of apocalypse, are possibly afraid? The pall clots, a sharpness at the temples. The sky pretends at simple. I have no quarrel with figments. Night garden, whetstone, small alien ships of seedpods tangled on the barbed wire. Here is the skull of the hummingbird on a chain around my neck. Let us pretend it's fleshed, the chain a leash; let us be sad souls who keep bones on silver threads. In the theater, the couple in the next row masturbated each other in the dark, dove noises as the city burned. After, I drove into the hills, past the reedy underbrush that pretends at fire. I hiked on; the pall did not dissolve, though I felt a little better, thank you.

Here the trailhead; here the sagebrush; here the creek, the glass house on the cliff, the telephone wires, the dust kicked up so that I am never without my vials of eye drops—"thinking for hours together of having the knife she gave me put in a silver-case—the hair in a Locket—and the Pocket Book in a gold net"—the absences tangible as hummingbird skulls. Having come to the trailhead, I crave *a speechless place caught up in a gold net.*

Grit in my teeth and the sky about to tear, I peer into the cleft two boulders make. Eye to the dark, I hear impossible water. I am learning to allow for visions. The cliffs give up a sound like howling, which merges with actual howling to become a system of enormous potential. A lightninged thicket; a road sliced out of winter; a tooth buried in the bark of a tree; a bowl of lathed yew; a ewe split like a peach but still bleating. I walk and walk. Like a jellyfish or annunciation, the heliodore-yellow underlying everything shimmers, is gone.

Often when I wake the furniture's slightly haloed, sleeping pill screwing with the visual cortex, a pleasant holiness. I believe he went home with her smell on his fingers; I believe that on the trail are many handsome dogs. The acedia hums and hums. Soon, excess and magnolia, snow in the mountains moving toward us as runoff, great volumes of water pulled into the valley, swans on the riverbank drinking that snow. I will sit by the trail until my head stops hurting. I will try not to be afraid.

# THE NIGHT GROVE

The torturer wants to know
how one minute blood, one minute
snow. She wants the windows
closed. The draft. Light breaks
across his back.




She lets the torturer put his head in her hands.
Tells him about Flanders,
the speaking dead.
*We are the Dead,* they say.
Where snow falls
in the taxonomy of the greater and lesser
desires: it falls on the taxonomy. On the money
and on the torso. On the fur.




She tells the torturer:
first, for practice, they bayonetted
straw men. Missing their villages, winter
descending. And then
the soft flesh of stomachs
attached to bodies
tied to trees.
He says,
that is a very ancient story.

She says, Simon Peter stirred the fire. There
in his animal body.
Yes, he says. Breath milk-warm
on her neck.


She says, maybe this weekend
we could flay the flesh from your back.


When she takes him inside
and through her body, what
is expiated? Nothing
is expiated. She tells him
of the torturer's horse.
He says: I was the horse and
I was his rider. She says:
and you were the body
quartered behind.


She says, some boys on the news
shot a swan.

She says, maybe you could start a book club
where you read about faith
systems. He stacks coins
on her belly
until it's difficult to breathe.

Gethsemane was more than
a garden, she says. People that night
dreamt of you. He
is weeping again but also
erect again.

She says, the dead swan. Their
daddy's rifle. Wings
eight feet wide.

"The way fear looks like anger in the animal's
dark eye"
is one way to narrativize
the universe.
Go ahead, he says.
Why not.

She says, or maybe you could start a support group
where horses ride over
your bodies. Those who survive
get to attend the next meeting.

She twirls the hair on his stomach.
The way freezing persons recollect the snow is
*they're sitting in the motherfucking snow*, the snow
is in their mouths and their eyes
are sealed by crystals.
What, then, of *outliving*?

Poppies are the flower of forgetting.
The old men outside the grocery store
pin one to his lapel.

She says, I want to hold those boys
close, and then
I want to shatter their finger bones.

See, he says?

# RIVER WALK

When the other world enters this one, she hears a little click. Day damp with the breath of other animals, hyperarousal of air on skin, everything yes and eyes and windows—

And sometimes day goes like: the soldier in class who's storing up food. The way the soldiers always sit nearest the door. The soldier who said he forgot he had legs and when she said, "then you woke up?" he said, "no, I was awake the whole time."

Walking home, river clotted with cottonwood dander, she avoids looking in the milky eye of the goat, too tired to make contact with any living thing.

Scientists say there is another planet just like ours except it is on fire.

On this planet, to show where the boy has gone, someone moves two fingers across the desk:

the boy is on the run.

Generally speaking, the riverbank's a good place for weeping.

She fantasizes that, when finally the hours are nothing so much as a horse rearing back, nostrils flared with pepper, she'll lower her head, she'll say

*Enough.*

The rug in the corner thick with poppies, the river thick with leaves; the light making a sort of medallion on the floor—

She'll renounce the medallion.

*She wakes with bruises stippled on her left*
*breast, and last month*
*a cyst that swelled, ceased, swelled; a fish*
*hook sunk into her thigh; a barb*
*under the nailbed from this invasive*
*thing that sheds, she*
*reads, 8,000 seeds per plant; a republic*
*that will not face its sins; a timid*
*lover, his blood sick with liquor. To wake*
*is masochism, would you*
*like to pay her very little*
*to edit something, or feed her, as*
*she kneels here, something sweet*
*which will, as years accrete, accrete along*
*the walls? The pinpoint*
*bruises turn her tit to art. To punish*
*herself, she doesn't even own a passport.*

To show that she is real, she walks the river path.

Feathers or fur?
Touch it with a stick.

*Strapping young buck go on your way*
*I have no minnows for you today*
*I have no grains no lace no moss and lie on a bed of*
*bridge, that is*
*on the footbridge lie and look and re-lume*
*by looking?*
*no*
*and breathe breath back into the swan by wishing?*
*no*
*and evade a relation of use?*
*no*
*don't think so*
*strapping young buck not buck but boy a-rifled*
*smooth-skulled where antlers aren't*
*go the fuck away*


To know that she is real, she walks the river path.
Legs grown stronger?
Working on her anger.


*She imagined a tent by the sea/imagined*
*the levitation of feathers/the dead swan*
*came to her in a dream/she walked*
*by the river/walked in the foothills*
*what she thought was a boy screaming*
*turned out to be a bird*
*what she thought was a bird*
*turned out to be sorrow*
*what she thought sorrow*
*was only a punishment*
*for making the world real*
*she could not make a clean shape of things*

*the river swirled fantastically*
*someone fed her venison as foreplay*
*someone tied a blue string around her wrist*
*milk of lovingkindness*
*no one will believe any of this*


To know that she is real, she watches the goat stand on hind legs to eat a flower.

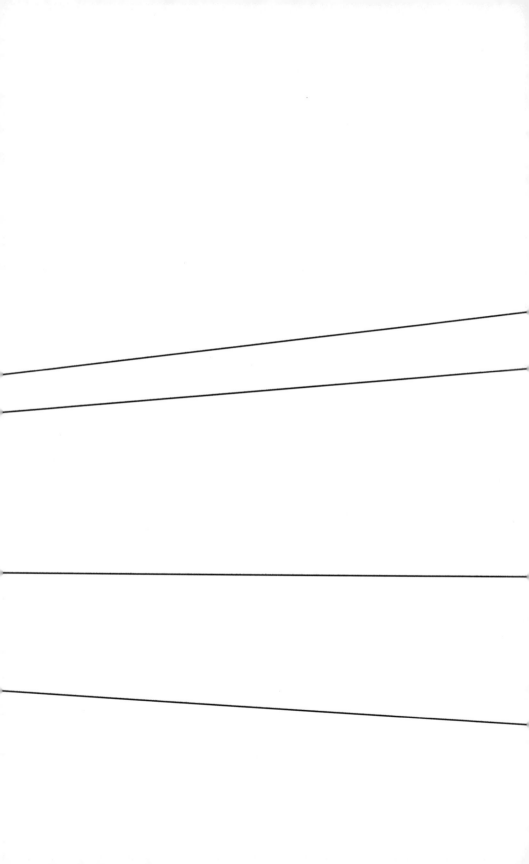

PART II

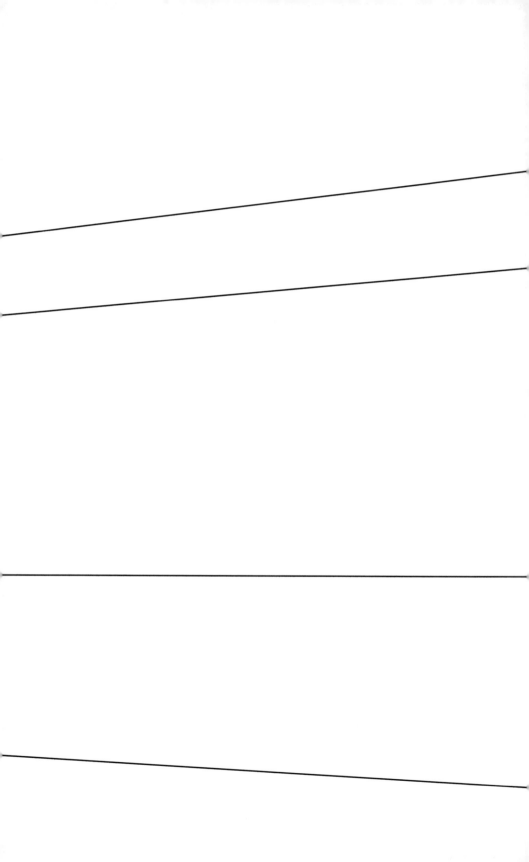

# WINTER OF
# (AND I TOOK THE CHEMISE OFF)

And I said to him You are such an atomist

and I took the chemise off

the canal had a scrim of green

there were bulb flowers underground

there was a tent glowing by the sea

it was that kind of quickstep reality

I felt I had reached the edge of myself
I felt that I spilled over
I felt it was not beautiful
I felt I was not beautiful
my soul stretched thin as a catalpa pod

and I said Remember those meteorite knives
in the shop in the very wet city

and he said No
I never saw them    I was never there
and I realized I was alone in this

have I mentioned how I don't know how to swim
have I mentioned how I type with one hand

the trees were hardcore gravure
against the muddy sky
and a sort of eclipse coming on
I was not ready
winter of light and

winter of feathers leaking out and
winter of berries red against filthy sky and
winter of Where'd your mind go
and ropes of velvet
ropes of velvet for tying up the hush
and I said Eyeless, and so terrible
which weren't my words at all
the light disorienting
the trail muddy
I walked and walked
put your body back on
put your body back on and let's go walking
and I said You with your particality
while I try to make of my mind a workable whole
and I said Hey atomist
well you know they've smashed that thing
everything swirling like propolis
filling up the spaces
filling up the light
sealing up the house
until no draft came through
and I took the chemise off

# CONVERSION NARRATIVE

*That was the season I felt uneasy in all my rooms. Having dragged nearly all the furniture out of the house*


<u>fine isolated verisimilitudes are terrifying</u>


*I was at that time dating an officer of the law called Officer Cocksure; was trying to erase narrativity by staring at a certain tree in Tower Grove Park till time dissolved. This was before protesters were tear-gassed by the park, before suburban boys back West started donning cowboy hats to announce their white nostalgia and their shortcomings all in one hat*


Someone said, *God is historical in the sense that God is rhetorical—the product of the language used to speak about God.*


The hydrangeas grew prehistorically large


My God-syntax went from imperative to interrogatory


I remember a girl screaming on the clinic floor—water feature out front aping beauty—her shrieks shattering the follicles of my right ear—the koi gaping—I wanted to kneel beside her on the stained carpet and say Yes. Exactly. All of us

*That was the season I felt uneasy in all my rooms. Having dragged nearly all the furniture out of the house so that when company came, no place to sit— embarrassing, and cannot say why I did this;*

I would walk the alleys looking for alley glass; would put the alley glass in jars; would set the jars on the sill; the spirit would enter the jars—

Language dissolved as it left people's mouths.

<u>first you are present then you are terrified</u>

*Officer Cocksure was pretty*

AROUND THIS TIME I found on a Free Cart a set of flashcards variously titled: How Satellites Will Change Your Life    Superstitious? Here's Why!    The Struggle for the World    Literature as Role-Playing    Your Voice Gives You Away    How to Handle the Sun    The Beginning of the Healing Art    The Girl Castaway    Can a Free Society Survive?    Does the Moon Influence Your Moods?    Quo Vadis, America?

*The koi were also pretty*

I was superstitious mainly because someone, either God or a desert fore-mother, kept talking to me in the dark. And the moon *was* my moods.

I felt a great power gathering/did not yet know this was MERCY: for the mad girl ushered out of the room, the boy who tied the string around my wrist, etcetera


Often I'd sob in the sculpture garden


*That was the season I felt uneasy in all my rooms. Having dragged nearly all the furniture out of the house so that when company came, no place to sit— embarrassing, and cannot say why I did this; only that my cells were readying—*


The alley glass appeared fire-formed


When the sun is hard to handle, you buy blackout curtains at Target, you stay in bed


*Officer Cocksure was a breast man, though of course I was not destined to date the State*


Holding class on the lawn near the arch that looked out over the 1904 World's Fair, language left: <u>my voice gave me away</u>, letters lifting off the page as bats did, from the dusk-pinked turrets


Having never lived in a free society

WHERE THE FAIR WAS HIPPOS NOW SWAM, sometimes lifting their great nostrils above water


[To whom or to what did my lapsed voice give me]


*That was the season I felt uneasy in all my rooms. Having dragged nearly all the furniture out of the house so that when company came, no place to sit— embarrassing, and cannot say why I did this; only that my cells were readying— and though no one else may say I was mad, I can say I was mad, and that when I returned—*


Alley glass threw blue-green shadows on the wall. And violent red


<u>first you are present then you are terrified then you are transformed</u>


Next door, a pit bull lived out his life on a second-story balcony, piss dripping down through the slats; of those humans and Mercy, I will only say that sometimes in hindsight it seems misplaced


*Gradually I became aware that both God AND the desert foremothers thought it silly that I lived outside of the sight of wilderness*


TOWER: a water tower
GROVE: no there was not
PARK: when a society abandons the pastoral, it demarcates lawn

*One of Officer Cocksure's duties was to enforce park curfew*


Rhetorical can mean:
- without expectation of answer
- with expectation of persuasion


TOWER: will crumble
PARK: swallowed by its own grasses
GROVE: we must maintain hope for the groves actual, the groves imaginary


*That was the season I felt uneasy in all my rooms. Having dragged nearly all the furniture out of the house so that when company came, no place to sit— embarrassing, and cannot say why I did this; only that my cells were readying— and though no one else may say I was mad, I can say I was mad, and that when I returned—soul clicking back into place, pineal gland starting up again—everything in this world became easier: leaving a lover; traffic; bodily illness; poverty—*


I loaded up the car, dragged what wouldn't fit into the alley


I paid my last respects to the trembling State


In someone's basement, a lemon tree produced three lemons in the dark

The hippos pressed their large eyes to the glass.

## OF DEBORAH

Deborah was a prophetess.
She sat under a palm tree
and knew what you're doing tomorrow.
All around, armies.
Cities burned etcetera.
Tomorrow you're buying pants.
Deborah's a terrible name for a prophetess.
Chariots, she says, sucking a plum stone.
Scorpions and nettles.
Toy guns in gumball machines.
Deborah wonders what's prophecy, what's
merely obvious.
Drought, she says, her throat drying out.
She knows the man will have the tent-pin
jammed into his skull, chooses
not to warn him. Who am I
to re-route history, says Deborah, employing
the metaphor of the stone in the current.
The goat wanders off.
Deborah sees the wires running under everything,
knows there's a mouse in your cistern.
To be a prophetess is to witness
world's end *ad nauseum*:
a sailor of less than average cognitive acumen
bashes the Dodo's skull with a rock,
the seas rise, a widow
doesn't make love for ten years.
Most of the things the kings ask Deborah
are fuckwitted things:
*Should I start a war?*
*Should I go to the war already begun?*
Deborah washes their questions
from between her legs.
Iron chariots shake the ground.
This is a tiny shitbox of land, she says, gesturing

towards the desert.
Evening and the mountains are melting again.
Deborah knows all zealots are boymen.
*Awake, awake, Deborah: awake, awake,*
*and utter a song:*
so she sings about how, when the waters retreat,
dreck gathers at her door.
She also has a very good song about monkeys,
and one about righteous acts.
Deborah reaches out to catch the bowl of plums
before it begins falling.

## REASONABLE MIRACLES

I too have loved furry men, I too have lost them.
The hills pink up fantastic.
And the vodka in its mason jar:
more theophany than this lady's used to.
Wind a blue powder on my skin, I lie on my belly
to feel the bridge as men ride over.
A man lifts, throws, lifts, throws
bottles into community recycling.
I hear the separate colors as they break.

# THE SPINSTER PROJECT

Spinster loves you. In her house. With her teeth.

Spinster's busy. Called, squints letters into shapes.

Spinster whistles her blue dog back from the bluedark woods.

Spinster is having a Vision! so (please) leave her be.

Spinster's house is smaller than your house, and your house, and yours yours yours.

Watching Criminal Minds, Spinster is glad she never married a sexual sadist who keeps eyeballs in Kerr jars.

Other creatures Spinster's never lawfully wedded: the State; Deans of Humanities; bank accounts; 6 a.m.

Spinster goes around all day thinking *vitreous humor* as she looks and looks.

Spinster considers writing a manifesto about authority, but Spinster *is* authority.

Spinster owns time and slices it like the sweetest pear tartlet.

Spinster "sleeps with monsters" and June's been quite the manticore, heavy-pawed muse trundling through her sleep—

To stay fully Spinstered, Spinster has an IUD. By night she sings to the egg as it leaves her body: Hallelujah little egg! Godspeed little you in your fine blood-apparel! Adios my sweet petite iron-tanged bomb-to-nowhere!

Spinster's bleary from staying inside your book for so long, but thank you.

Spinster adores her some pink lingerie.

Spinster is standing in the desert. The desert is standing around Spinster. They exchange molecules.

Spinster thought of having an imaginary daughter, but the thinking made her tired. Within minutes she was leaving her imaginary daughter on the orphanage steps, note pinned to her sweater signed, Fondly, yr Spinster.

Spinster knows she's becoming an erratic, a boulder left by retreating ice.

Spinster's new lover has bought her a diamond. Ruh-roh, says Spinster to the white dog, their brows furrowed in cross-species commiseration.

It's possible that Spinster is secretly the taxidermist of your hopes and dreams.

There's a covert op designed to unSpinster Spinster. It's code name is TheWholeFuckingHistoryoftheWideWideWorld.

Spinster knows her breath is a mimetic representation of clouds, clouds a meontic representation of mystery, a barely-there of the there-but-where.

In the movie where Spinster hangs herself from the tree because Spinster, Spinster knows as soon as the swinging blue corpse enters the frame that the screenplay was written by a man.

Spinster wants to literalize your desire inside her mouth.

Spinster pawns her watch to buy herself a hair comb, her hair to buy herself a watch chain. Bald, she hangs the comb from the chain and proceeds clangingly.

In all seriousness, Spinster knows she has gotten born at exactly the right moment in exactly the right place, knows there are a few billion girls who cannot construct a Spinsterhood, girls who—denied their Spinster destinies as soon as blood starts to leak from them—may choose to set themselves on fire.

Spinster needs an epoch to think about that.

Spinster resolves to Spinster better harder faster. In the phraseology of her childhood, she has the technology.

Spinster kills what botanists say even a monkey could water.

In a rare but pleasing meeting of word origin, insect (sort of), and kismet, *Spinster* is suggestive of spinning, of weaving, as per spider, as per web, hence many last names.

Spinster concubines the whiskey. Spinster courtesans the empty lot. Spinster jezebels the very air until it is much more interesting air.

Spinster considers that the original Spinsters were holy women—that to declare Full Spinster you'd show up at God's embassy, ask for asylum, and wait to be let in.

Spinster knows that all paths, if chosen, are gorgeous, but secretly feels it's no coincidence that our greatest poet was a Spinster.

Spinster does not think she is holy in the manner of, say, rivers or Radioactive Wolves, but maybe a little holy.

Spinster drives home pleasingly fucked/lies down in the backyard, looking up.

Spinster worries she is becoming an isolate, a language with no discernable roots.

Spinster licks the peach juice off her hand.

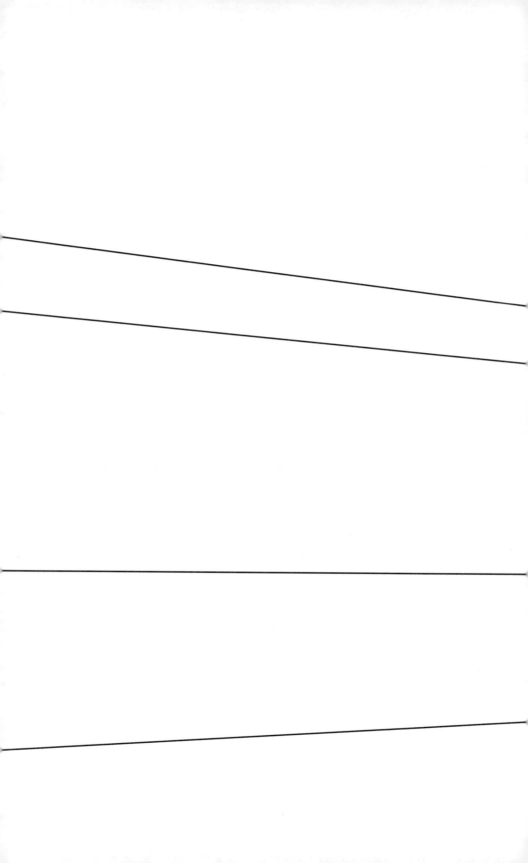

PART III

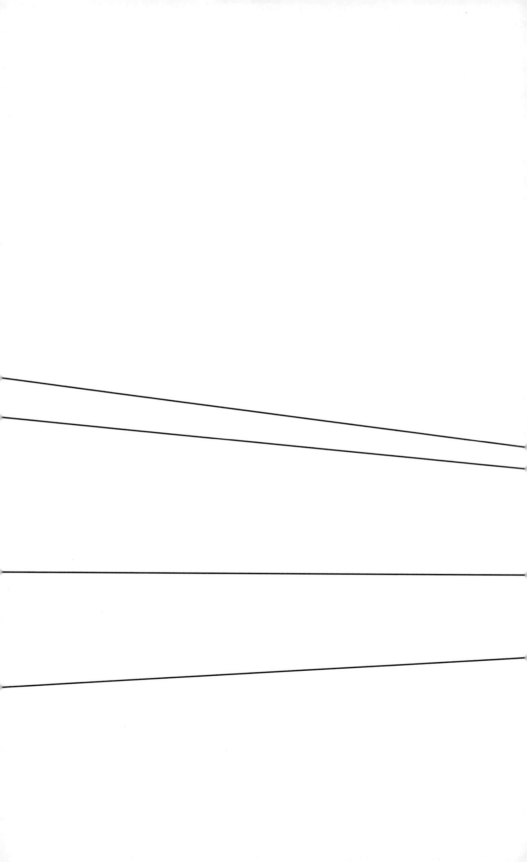

## THIS IS MANIFEST

What I needed to survive was, currents
moving over my body.
Also, bourbon.
Saw a light through the trees:
serum? Lantern?
Baby, I said to the man kneeling
between my legs, there are kit foxes out there
and they hum when they learn a new thing
like ledges or stream-fording.
For years my soul was little more than an embassy.
I was lush, and then lush, and then more lush.
In all of my opening, who had I actually saved?
I was no one's bodhisattva. And so
I removed my body from the systems.
Walked the hills by night.
My blisters filled with sticky fluid.
A swan made a freakishness of its neck.
I was a woman of such secret knowledge
as you may think mad.
I don't know why, when we die,
all our skulls aren't jeweled.
Sometimes I was so enamored of sky
I felt my milk might come in.

# SWAN/NOT SWAN

Girl in the wilderness, what does she know?
Gray dress bought for how it looks
unbuttoning—
you have heard this story before.
Oh we are sorely fugitive and lapsed
from our better selves.
If we are pretty ghosts, hammered in—
scraped out and sobbing in cars, I want
to sleep and sleep.
The leaves sprouting over my breasts, the tongue
pushing them away—
in the dark I am not the dark.
In the quiet I am not the quiet
violence of snow.
Pheromones from heartbreak only cashier-men
can smell: they touch
too much my hands.
A woman's no amphora.
I feel ALL RADIUM, ALL NOVA.
Honey I am no gazelle, am not into pony play, am
investigating mercy—
what comes after we hurt each other.
In this season of lost light, I am walking
out of wilderness, a goddamned
lady Ishmael. As *heel*
is kin to its homonym, I go submissive
all October. What sleeps in the trees
chirps horribly along my spine as I,
kneeling, say: You darlings built of dread
and skin, who will build my sensory-
deprivation chamber now?
Having come to a topos where more's wanted
than suffer-flutter/suffer-thud;
intercessor-less;
immured in flesh;

nearing wet bulb temperature—
light gathers itself into pins.
We turn our violence into shapes—
a man, a swan, an alphabet—and see
how, in the beginning, the world was phosphorous
and singed our fur, and now
this planet made of sorrow
where the boy shoots the swan, opens
a portal in its chest which his soul
enters and enters and enters
again. Girl in the wilderness, what does she know?
How *mean* means both cruel and small.
What comes after we hurt each other
is, we hurt each other more?
Cylinders of cold line this house
and I cannot get warm.
The actual worship-space was very small.
Mostly we practiced survival skills
and waited for the end. What comes after
we hurt each other?
It gets really quiet.
We do or do not get out of bed.
Like birds there comes an astonishment of
kindnesses.
Hello.
Hello.
Light slams into snow.

## ONE EYE DILATED

Months of one eye dilated, light flooding in, a constant low-grade headache. I feel, in conversation, asymmetrical, and want to look away, yet also know it to be beautiful, like the husky across the street (green/blue) or the burned-down church next to the standing church.

From this new fixity/the dilated eye: how much light there is (a lot); how our bodies in their mercy keep us from it. The dilated thing is made in its own expanded image. Time dilation is when another's clock moves more slowly than your own, which is unfair, because then that person gets more of everything. The cervix is dilated when the intrauterine device is inserted.

The following questions are suggested post-eclipse: *Describe what you observed. What, if anything, surprised you? What would you do differently? Why? What are the umbra and penumbra?*

I walk past the woodpecker tree, the sound like the insistence of light on the eye.

Often when I'm speaking, or listening, I'm speaking, yes, or listening, but also, from the pain, acutely aware of looking—your mouth, moving; what rests above your shoulder (in the distance, river)—looking become pilgrimage, eye travailing this long desire for rest, but no rest, just a sharp stab along the optic nerves.

*What, if anything, surprised you?*

I am loud inside myself, but from an exterior perspective not so much.

Sometimes I wish to put my eye out; the sky will not cease its pour and there seems no true darkness, just as there seems no true silence; they say that even the giraffes are humming, the mice are singing. The giraffes are humming, the trees are communicating, I cannot sleep and find I've forgotten to breathe. The way the body says so is by gasping.

*What would you do differently?*

For years I tried to worry the world into containment, even as the condom got lost inside me or something blotted out the sun.

It has taken me forever to be obedient to the beautiful, rather than the easy, things.

# TOWARDS AN ETHICAL RELIGIOSITY

*Brothers, above the starry canopy*
*There must dwell a loving father.*
*World, do you know your creator?*
—Friedrich Schiller, "Ode to Joy"

Do not say I am insensible. Here is the demon trapped under glass, and here I am, demiurge of the simulacrum, having given him universe within universe: ground (carpet), sky (jarred air), and above, this heaven through which I move unfettered, buying lubricants, eating pomegranates, each return to the windowless room revealing him still here, my rash action perhaps once its own apologia yet this is no longer that; grown deliberate, the truth is I am afraid, amygdala by coincidence or design about the size of him and lit, his body coded in my genome, become muscle memory the way, when I've come for a man once, I come more readily for him again, control being thus illusion, yes? What is good and what is craven war inside me, given as I am to sensate bondage, profligate, sugared, respondent to the slightest touch. I type long into the night, let beloveds enter as blips of light, drink too much wine. Perhaps he is unkillable; perhaps, as my desert foremothers swore, he possessed a pre-mortal existence to which he will return—and if he feels no hurry, who among us can fault him? Sweet realm of stars and honey—

And now he drags one leg.

And now I leave ajar the door lest we be trapped together here.

He thrives and thrives. I worry my desire, finger the gap between want and have. He breathes, an honest act; I feign contentment so as not to seem ungrateful for what excess the hour provides. He harms—despite my fear—no one, while I giantess through space and time, clumsying up the realm, failing to love as the universe commandeth, disobedient—oft-liquored—superfluous to the ecosystem or, at very best, its consort. He curls into a galaxy and will not die. On the news, the women sing to the women over the prison walls: *Daughters of Elysium*: and in my thralldom I begin to feel companioned by what I've maimed.

# SKINS

**1.**
Here is the swan splayed dead
on the bed of the pickup truck, massive
wings blue-tinged—odd,
but I don't know enough about light
to decode what I see.

**2.**
When people call a woman
*shy*, they generally mean
*afraid*, translating quiet
to a comfortable thing.

**3.**
The trees slough off blue skins.

**4.**
When the boy who had done impossible harm
tied the string around my wrist,
he tied the world's sorrow around my wrist.
It burned like hell.
I feel it still, and don't
know what to do.

**5.**

In the image, the swan's a gross curvature
among lawn tools.

**6.**

I ruin my shoes in the river
where the swan was shot
by boys on the riverbank,
our cruelties like mercury
passed palm to palm.

**7.**

The skins of trees
pool around my feet.

**8.**

Rain and the river
swollen beside campus
where students with *enhanced permission*
bring guns to class.
I pretend the satellites are ancient
to get through this grammar.

**9.**

The river goes see-through.

**10.**

Over lunch, we discussed the loneliness
of men. I ate
the killed animal
among the leaves.

# INVERT SKY

I poke the wound of steadfast longing with this switch pulled from the creek. A man puts my hair in his mouth. What I want is to sit across the table from women and sop our bread in oil. The antlers on the bench build a pretty thicket. I am willing the days to be quiet, delusion of snow and echo, stupendous become end us, awful become full. Meat dissolves into broth. The first wound was contrition. The second wound was compassion. Someone painted a constellation in this bowl and I support that decision, I do, though beauty is more often brutal. Naked at midnight I throw stones at the animals who would disembowel my animals. The milk shoots straight from the saint's breast into the beggar's mouth. The chapter headings read The Body in Space, The Abject Body, The Body Absent. I take my body along the trail. Quartz in the stream. I was sorry, and then I felt too much, and then I could not stop longing. I bite my nails, swallow the keratin. Pica: the body knows what it needs. Chalk and drywall, potassium and mercy. When I pretended not to have a body, I wasn't very free.

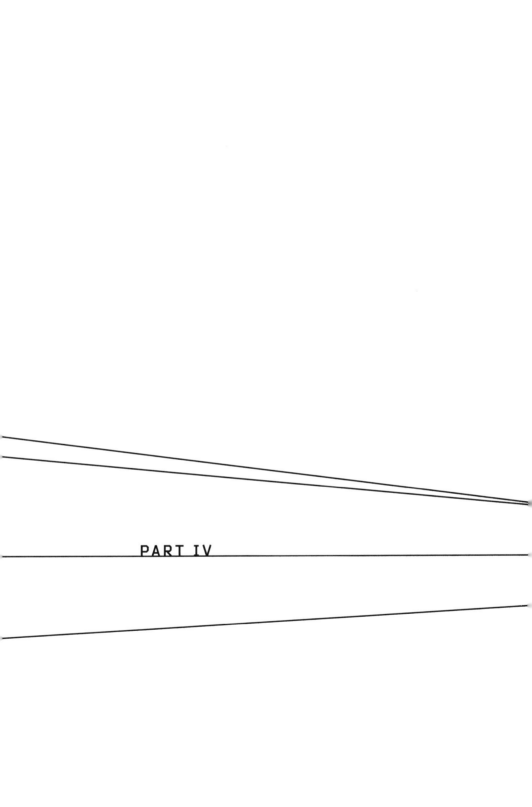

PART IV

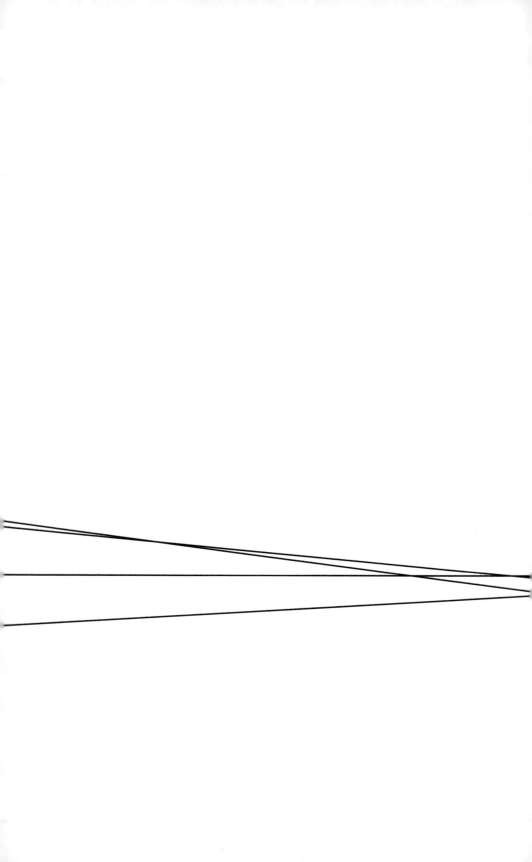

# WILDERNESS, POETRY, SEX

: red grasses underwater
flat with the weight of water
also a blue and yellow oar
also a blue spot on the river floor
maybe a portal


stone cold sober I say to you
for years a connoisseur of
pleasure then cast those
fellows out      and now
when people ask after my lusts
I do yes awayward
: towards the sagebrush
: towards the petroglyphs
: towards the feed lots where
through slats in the pens
a dark eye, a dark eye, a dark eye


the passions move through us
like phosphorous
burning away the subtleties
burning away the nonsense


having called the kind custodian
to mop up the flood
having locked myself in the ugly building
to get some poetry done
I a decadent lady


the body in space, the abject body

the body's limits, the absent body


us like phosphorous


I live at the edge of the
desert              the screen
sears my "bad" eye
which lets in too much
light/


AND THEN I SLEPT


*to the cosmic are we transparent*
said the holy whore/


AND THEN I SLEPT


when you see through to essence
: say, come three times in a row
how jarring, this travelling
back from the kingdom of desire
which was also the kingdom
of suffering so that
for months I pushed
over the hills
a Sorrow Cart


sorrow sorrow!
sorrow sorrow!

boots muddied


and the Lord said of pure light
*You will not be able to see it*
*as long as you are carrying flesh around*
I think this is because
he was not a woman
and so limited in experience
as per when I wade into the river
or, what a really good cock can do
or how, in the desert,
the metal signs [NO
SHOOTING] [WESTERN
HERITAGE] [SCENIC BYWAY] are
shot up
by boys with rifles and
then
the sky
pours
through


not to mention the non-literal signs


we the all of us do not know our righteous labor


the body in space, the penetrated body


the body's limits, the excelsiored body


there was a mountain called Divination and Joy

I lived there, begettress of mercy, one uber-palpable lady

and took my excess on down the trail

and waited for the owls to call

# SOLASTALGIA

Say the terrain. Somewhere between Exclusion Zone
and Asphodel Meadows. Drop-
dead gorgeous.
Through mourning we came to believe
in transformation—the way Tiresias
was blind, then dead, then seven years a woman.
An aunty said:
*Now everything is changing, even*
*the trees, you can see changes*
*in them, even the fruits, like before, we*
*haven't had mango season.*
And indeed we had not had mango season
in a long goddamned time.
And indeed we turned around and where
spiky mountains loomed now loomed
vast fields of air.
And indeed you too can be seven years a woman.
And indeed I sent my lovers away.
And indeed the last Pyrenean Ibex vanished and
you, you didn't even notice, nor did I notice, for I
was busy. And indeed
the lamp's burnt out.
Whoever said I was brave?
Nobody said is who.
Her name was Celia.
The ibex's name was Celia.


I stay where I am because other places frighten me.
Where the rivers come together in ghost-flowered banks,
only Tiresias thinks clearly.
What kind of blessing is that?
Man-sorrow made me an idiot.
I looked down and the wilderness had othered

into wildfire. And we read the signs—yesiree—we
knew—but:
what good is divination?
"Some languages may specialize in melancholy, or
seaweed, or
atomic structure, or religious ritual."
They took Celia's cells and made
another Celia, but New Celia's lungs
would not bellow and unbellow properly.
I am weeping for New Celia.
I am shedding cognitive dissonance like a veil
made of rain.
In the smoke-shapes, Tiresias divined
burning fleets, ghost leviathans, stadiums
filled with wandering shades, and abandoned towns
with Radioactive Wolves, which is also the name
of an excellent documentary.


*Say the terrain.* Somewhere between Superfund site
and Paradiso. Bitter-
pretty. All winter searching
for first principles, smoke in my hair
and my aporia a holstered knife. And if
I withhold punishment, which is
what mercy means?
I watch again the animated map of wind.
I drive into the desert and let the sky
abrade my skin. Seven years
a woman, now again
a man, Tiresias in all his loveliness remembers
the underworld, suitors
squeaking like bats.
Imagines he still has breasts
and plays with them.
Closes his eyes and sees
the world at wet bulb temperature, degree

at which we no longer expel wet heat
so cook inside our skins.
Some languages specialize in excoriation, or
squid metaphors, or
pre-mourning. In her bones
she knew the end of things, knew
the body's immolation
and all the lovers grown old, sorrow
terraforming into mythos
even as we stand here.

# CORPSE FLOWER

June and the woman ties the blindfold
around my eyes, leads me up a hill.
Someone calls to tell me about the immaculate
Ferragamos of the dead. The grove
unseen grows wilder than the grove
made visible. Bark rough as punished skin,
beetles shimmy up the vascular. Thrall,
not thrall—all I want is to sit in the dark
and not be the film about the lady
empath. Air a message sewn into our
hems, daylight bruits against my bad eye.
The lady empath bleats, swoons. *You*
*could smell it from the parking lot.* Spadix
wrapped in spathe, right, ladies?
Blooms one day a year. Let wolves
suck marrow from the bones of boys.
The aspens clone themselves. I take
my clothes off. The cormorants come
back. A star burns out. At Meteora,
monks line the old monks' skulls on ledges.
I slide my underwear down. Someone
sets food out for his dead—ribeye,
soda, plum. I unhook my bra. My
breasts spill out. The ceiling fan
cuts heat into districts. Head on his
chest. The aquifer quivers in the dark.
At Stuttgart, at Basel, at Kagoshima,
they open up the gardens long
into the night, and the crowds come.

# ON THE NATURE OF RIGHTEOUS ACTION

One. It is relentless. Two. Exhausting. Three. SCARY.

I am speaking the holy language of the future.

Evening and the mountains are melting again.

Who would ask for such power?

A man puts his head in my hands.

The dog wheels in the field, torques the chain around its neck.

And the woman said: *If grain is worth eating, it is worth eating before winter.*

I put my mouth and.

Discrete yet sharing and.

Sacralization is when things become holy, also when vertebra fuse.

I never want the cherry in the whiskey, I want the bitters.

The burning house floats down the river.

The lonely boy says the government's coming for his guns.

I keep encountering women who believe my soul is lost.

And if I am a burned-over district.

And if I crawl.

And if I am a little lost, out clipping lettuces—

WHAT IF what we call scrupulosity is actually the face of God revealed in what repeats but not revealed until the motion stops — and then we see?

And what if I'm afraid to stop?

There are levels of the kingdom
doctrine and covenant say I cannot enter.

The bugs shatter against the light.

Prayer that all things be done extravagantly, fruit sucked down to its stone—

And the woman said: *Let us consume the greens of the field*
*for they are drizzled in bacon fat.*

The ancestors speak in tongues.

What if I'm *sealed* to the world and have, yes, secret names
only lovers know?

And what if, when they call, I choose not to answer?

It has taken years to bring me to obedience.

And if I am mercenary with my time, how then
to be more mercenary?

Honeysuckle trellises the bedframe.

"Have you lived sufficiently"

The sky itself a salvific mystery

I slip outside ordinary time/live there a while/slip back in

The mind, lenticular, traces the river out of town, touches
the birds as it goes, touches
the mites on the wings

## THE TRAILHEAD

I have acquired a piece of luggage even smaller than the last.
Eventually I will own only silver and a pen.
I am no lunar denier, mean only
that I have embarked on
an era of lesser exploration
which I record in a commonplace
labeled Excelsior.

# VANITAS

Striated stones returned to the wrong river, blue house
falling into the sun, the systems refusing to be allegory—
when I was fully present I thought presence would
kill me, vines forcing through windows and the soul-
sucking slowing of time when I broke inside. Here
is your weighted blanket, here is your poppy, I know
a woman just waiting for elegy to show up in her brain,
alive only for that, and then she can go. I pretend
form will save us, worry about how much the reiterative
soothes me, stones lined on the sill so my mind
stays still in this realm. Here is the landmass tattooed
on my body, here are the flowers we've planted
to cover up what we've done, creeping myrtle, creeping
phlox, creeping thyme, none of this easy, what with
the man shoving the girl's face into the ground,
what with the world burning down, creeping alyssum
shock-yellowing the yard, sea of stems pinning down
absolutely nothing. Daily I wake inside expiation's
failure, bee brooch pinned to my breast instead of
a cross, testament to the foolishness of placing pleasure
before all we could not bear, our souls the color of
propolis but our monkey hearts marbled with folly.
The way a command can also be a plea: *Fuck me,*
the imperative our truest tense because who doesn't want
to top from bottom, really, rule and abdicate
all in one breath? I know a widow who didn't make
love for ten years, slow death my mind can't grasp,
glancing then glancing away. The air tastes of sugar and
my hilly body's one hell of a gateway and when I first
saw the statue of the great god Pan, I wanted very much
to mount him, lick that sweet spot where pelvis meets
furry haunch. I gray splendid, I come in palms, and
I would never, ever be a girl again, despite all the years'
terrible knowledge. We move through these long last days
*touched*, which is to say fingered, which is to say moved,

which is to say mad. The stranger carves a gold tunnel
through the gold book. The river faces up neon, glows and
glows. I set my glasses by the bed, walk the river path.
Show me the gold tunnel. Show me where the gold tunnel goes.

# NOTES

I.

"Hill Walk": "Cast him out at gates and let him smell his way to Dover" and "And cry these dreadful summoners grace?" are from *King Lear*.

"Hulls Gulch": "The only comfort I have had that way has been in thinking for hours together of having the knife she gave me put in a silver-case—the hair in a Locket—and the Pocket Book in a gold net—": John Keats, from a letter dated October 24, 1820.

"The Night Grove": The poem was inspired by the essay "Consequences" by Eric Fair, originally published in *Harper's*. "We are the Dead" comes from the poem "In Flanders Fields" by John McCrae. The poem also references Emily Dickinson.

"River Walk": "There is another planet just like ours except it is on fire" refers to an article by Phil Plait in *Slate* ("Exoplanet Is Earth's Burned-Out Molten Twin").

II.

"Winter Of (And I Took the Chemise Off)": "Eyeless, and so terrible" is Virginia Woolf's, from *To the Lighthouse*.

"Conversion Narrative": The quote "God is historical in the sense that God is rhetorical—the product of the language used to speak about God" comes from the Westar Institute's "Seminar on God and the Human Future."

"Of Deborah": Her story is told in the Bible, Judges.

"The Spinster Project": The phrase "sleeps with monsters" is Adrienne Rich's, from "Snapshots of a Daughter-in-Law."

# III.

"Swan/Not Swan": The poem uses lines from poems published between 1996 and 2013 but not collected in my earlier books. Thanks to *Denver Quarterly*, *Crazyhorse*, the *Indiana Review*, and the *Mid-American Review* for publishing those poems.

"One Eye Dilated": Italicized questions come from a National Geographic Society article titled "Build a Solar Eclipse Viewer."

"Invert Sky": The phrase "wound of steadfast longing" and the enumerated wounds come from Julian of Norwich's *Revelations of Divine Love*.

# IV.

"Wilderness, Poetry, Sex": The poem incorporates language from the Gnostic text "The Dialogues of the Savior."

"Solastalgia": The term was coined by Glenn Albrecht. In the poem by that title, the italicized portion beginning "Now everything was changing" is from the essay "Solastalgia and the Gendered Nature of Climate Change: An Example from Erub Island, Torres Strait," by Karen Elizabeth Mc-Namara and Ross Westoby. "Some languages may specialize . . ." is from the essay "Radical Linguistics in an Age of Extinction" by Ross Perlin.

"On the Nature of Righteous Action": "Have you lived sufficiently" quotes Martin Corless-Smith. Deepest gratitude to Martin, too, for the book's title.

## ABOUT THE AUTHOR

Kerri Webster is the author of the poetry collections *We Do Not Eat Our Hearts Alone* (2005) and *Grand & Arsenal* (2012), the latter of which won the Iowa Poetry Prize. The recipient of awards from the Whiting Foundation and the Poetry Society of America, she has taught at Washington University in St. Louis and Boise State University.